The $5 A Day Stock Market Program: A Guide to Black Wealth

By Dr. Boyce Watkins

CONTENTS

ACKNOWLEDGMENTS

I would like to thank everyone who has supported the work that we do to improve the lives of others.

CHAPTER 1

WHY THE STOCK MARKET?

There is this strange idea that somehow the stock market is only for "other" people or people who work for corporations who invest on their behalf. Starting right now, we need to stop giving credence to these ideas. They hurt us and our ability to produce generational wealth.

We need to think of the stock market as a space where we belong and that will benefit us. In order to do this, it is important to clarify what the stock market is, how it works, and how it will benefit you and your family.

Here are some key facts to think about. Trillions of dollars in wealth are being created on the stock market; the rich are getting richer. The reason the rich are getting richer is mainly because they own stocks and own businesses. In this mini-book, I want to emphasize the importance of owning stocks.

Traditionally, working and middle class people will aspire to buy homes. This is the bulk of their wealth. If you're middle class, a significant percentage of your wealth is in your home or maybe it is in your retirement. If you want to be upper class, you have to step your game up a notch. Instead of owning one home, wealthy people find a way to buy multiple homes and, most importantly, to invest.

Instead of working for people, they own companies. Instead of being an employee, they are employers. Additionally, their stocks earn money for them.

So that's how the rich get richer. That's what the 1% does. Middle class people own homes and poor people own nothing unfortunately. But there are ways to be an owner no matter who you are, no matter what your income level is. So what are some keys?

One of the persistent challenges being faced by the black community is the wealth gap. According to recent studies, black wealth and white wealth are hugely disproportionate. The last study I read indicated that white wealth was about 10 to 12 times higher than the median black wealth on a per capita, or family, basis.

One of the things I want to do is propose a solution to this problem. My Ph.D. is in finance and my dissertation was on the stock market so I know finance really well. Additionally, I taught finance for 23 years. After listening to people in our community express unawareness about the stock market, I thought it was time to offer a quick, accessible way to bring the stock market to your home.

It may not be a solution for everybody because not

everybody is going to do this even though the process is very basic. But for those of you who are willing, this guide will help set you up for success.

It's something that came to me literally in the middle of the night. I woke up and I wrote down some notes and said I have to talk to people about this. Basically it's the five dollar a day investment plan. Yes, you read that correctly; it is called *The five dollar a day investment plan.*

The good thing is that the process is painless. In fact, it doesn't take a lot of discipline to do this for most people. It doesn't have to be five dollars a day; it can be 50 dollars a day; it can be 15 dollars day; it can even be two dollars a day depending on what you choose. Regardless of the amount, the point is that you have to start with something. I'm choosing five dollars a day because it's easy to explain to people and it's easy to show the results.

As I have mentioned before in my videos, blogs, and with my students in my investments classes, it is important to understand why Albert Einstein once said that compound interest is the most powerful force in the universe. Once you understand it, you won't be afraid of it and you can watch it work in *your favor.*

Recently I did a video showing that, for example, if you spend a thousand dollars a month in rent, you are turning your landlord into a millionaire.

Here's how that works. Let's say that over a 25 to 30 year period, your landlord was investing that money in the stock market. At the conclusion of that time period, your landlord would have about 1.4 million dollars in extra wealth that he earned from the money that you gave him.

Some people might think that black people can't make themselves rich, but the reality is that you make a lot of other people rich just by paying rent. Just on rent alone, we are creating millionaires every single day. This is just using rent as an example; I can go into numerous other analogies. Don't get me started on stuff like "rent a centers" and other entities that exploit black communities.

My point is that I like this five dollar a day investment plan because almost anybody can do it. If you can afford a cup of coffee every day then you can do it. If you can afford to go to McDonald's once a week, you can do it. If you can afford to go to the movies once every couple of weeks, you can do it. If you can afford to go to the club, you can do it. If you can afford Jordan's, you can do it. If you can afford hair weaves, you can do it. If you can afford to give money to your pastor, you can do it. If you can afford money for clothes and going to the mall and Black Friday shopping, you can do it too.

This is something that almost everybody can do. It doesn't mean every single person. Maybe there's somebody out there who really can't afford it and that's fine. The point is not to make anyone feel bad about their current financial situation, but to help them improve it. If you don't have five dollars, but you have two dollars a day or one dollar a day then you can come together with family members and you all can invest five dollars.

Based on the history of the stock market, if you do

this then you will actually find yourself with a lot more wealth.

I'm going to do the math for you so that you can imagine and understand this. The first thing I want to explain to you is the wealth gap over time between whites and blacks. According to a recent study, Whites have about 144 thousand in wealth compared to maybe about 11,600 for black people.

The gap is pretty big. But this isn't really about catching up with white people, this is about contextualizing the problem so that you can understand the necessity of solving this problem on our own. It also helps to illuminate how we can solve it within a generation with very basic behavior and consistent codes of conduct—codes of economic conduct that advance our communities.

Let's imagine a calculator. This is what they call the future value of an annuity calculator. In my stock market investing class, we talk in great detail about how annuity's work, how compound interest works, the formulas and other important concepts and terms.

For now, it is simply important to note that there are various parameters that someone can use to predict earning outcomes. If I change the calculator to daily and I put in five dollars a day, it will commute the return on my investment (ROI). But, first, I have to add the type of annuity.

There are different types of annuity, including ordinary annuity and annuity due. Ordinary annuity is the most typical. Imagine that I put in nine percent as my annual interest rate. Why did I put in nine percent?

Because that's a reasonable rate of return that an investor would have gotten in the stock market over almost any 10, 20, or 30 year time period of American history.

For example, let's say I started this plan in 1992. By the year 2002, depending on the amount I invested, I would have *X amount of dollars*. Using that same premise, we guesstimate or extra calculate what will happen in 2026 or 2027 if we start in the year 2017 or right now.

Let's say that for 10 straight years you invest using a basic app. You might want to try an app like Stash, Acorns, or Robin hood. You put five dollars a day into your investment portfolio. A portfolio is a great idea because it will let you diversify your stock options. So many people get stuck on which stock to start with. Let me reassure you that even animals can build wealth.

There was actually an experiment that showed that if monkeys followed very basic investing strategies, they could actually build wealth. I'm not making that up. That's sounds crazy but they did an experiment with monkeys investing and picking stocks and the monkeys built wealth by randomly picking stocks. A more extensive examination of this study can be found in *A Random Walk Down Wall* by Burton Malkiel.

The book really helps to illustrate why picking a particular stock is not as important as actually investing to begin with. If a person wavers on investing because they can't decide on a stock then that is valuable time that is wasted—remember, time is your ally.

In the book, Burton does an experiment where he has

monkeys ·pick stocks, and basically the monkeys actually make more money than the experts from Wall Street and the reason is because monkeys don't make it complicated. The monkeys would just pick the stock and go eat bananas or whatever and let the stocks grow.

Here's why that actually makes sense. If you have five dollars a day and invest it for 10 years at nine percent interest, your money will grow. A person could be poor or making minimum wage, yet if they put five dollars a day toward their long term future, they will escape poverty.

How much money will they have in 10 years? That person would have $29,591.57. I want you to pay attention to another factor here. This is the power of compound interest. Out of that amount, the interest is $11,000. They made $11,000 just by investing—just by putting their money in the stock market, letting it grow, and going on with their lives.

You go to church and the pastor says if you put your money in the offering plate, the Lord will give it back to you ten fold, right? The same thing actually happens with stock market investing. When you put money in, you're getting money back. You're getting additional money back that you didn't even earn. How often in America does that happen?

This is why I push for us to seriously consider investing. It is one thing if we are unaware and don't know, but once we become aware, we have to act on that and we have to stop thinking that investing, the stock market, and wealth accumulation and managemet are not available to black America.

Not only is the stock market available to us, but it is one of the rare arenas were the playing field is relatively equal.

CHAPTER 2

HOW THE STOCK MARKET WORKS IN YOUR FAVOR

When our emphasis is on investing, our money literally grows for us and it's led to a concept that I came up with called economic fertility. When you invest, you allow your money to be fertile. You've allowed your money to reproduce itself the same way a bunch of bunny rabbits reproduce if you put them all in the same pen together.

Your money is supposed to have reproductive organs and not simply be sterile. Financial sterility is when you take your money and you kill it by giving it away and buying stuff with it. When you take that five dollars and, instead, invest that money using a basic app, you can actually multiply your wealth.

I use the bunny rabbit analogy because it helps people to visualize the process. Let's say your goal was to own as many rabbits as you possibly could, right? How would you accumulate a stockpile of rabbits? If they were $10 a piece, would you just go and buy 10 rabbits this week and then 10 more next week and 10 more the next week and just keep accumulating?

Then if you have $5,000 would you buy 500 rabbits at $10 a piece?

No, you don't do that. If you're smart, what you do is you buy five male rabbits and five female rabbits. You put them in a pen, you turn on some Marvin Gaye, and you let nature take its course. You let the rabbits create other rabbits. Then next thing you know, you've got rabbits on top of rabbits and then the rabbits that are born are getting together with other rabbits and making more rabbits.

Next thing you know, you've got 1,000 rabbits when you only started off with 10. Well, money grows like bunny rabbits. In a way, think of your money as money rabbits. Imagine this happening over many, many years because you're just doing the same thing every day—investing.

What happens is you create power. This creates financial power. When I first started sharing this information, I had a real hard time trying to convince black people that we can actually do something. We can actually build something because there's so many people who really believe that we're just broke and that's where we're supposed to be forever and it bothers me very much. So I sat around thinking about creative ways to help people understand how anybody, historically anyway, can build wealth if that's what they choose to do.

This is why $5 is my magic number. If you go to a coffee shop and you get a water and a banana, you're going to spend more than $5. If you get a large coffee and a muffin, you're going to spend about seven, eight, nine dollars or more.

Why not spend that money on something that works for you?

CHAPTER 3

SHIFTING FROM A POVERTY TO A WEALTHY MINDSET

Investing in the stock market will help a person shift from a poverty mentality to one of wealth. One of the first things to note is that a person who invests over a period of time is no longer poor. You could've started this plan as a poor person but in 10 years you're no longer poor. I don't know a single poor person who can say I have $29,591 dollars available in stock. That person doesn't exist because that person, as long as he/she lets the growth accumulate, is no longer poor.

Let's go deeper. Let me show you the beauty of compound interest. When investing, time is the most valuable asset you have. In other words, time is your ally.

Instead of doing 10 years, let's do 20 years. Let's imagine a person who invests for 20 years straight using the five dollar a day investment plan. How much money will they have in 20 years? In 20 years, that person will have $102,368 dollars. Once again, the power is in the details.

They put in $36,000 but interest brought home almost $66,000 dollars.

Interest gave them double the amount of money that they invested. For every dollar that they put in, they earned two additional dollars. Remember, this is the amount of money that many of us spend daily at Starbucks to buy one cup of coffee. Honestly, you can not even get a decent meal for five dollars at McDonald's. These days, you have to buy off of the dollar menu to get something to eat. You can't feed your family at McDonald's for five dollars—not that you should—I'm not judging you if you do eat at McDonald's. I'm just telling you the truth.

Investing in the stock market is a way out of poverty. In fact, some people, in one generation, have shifted because of long term investments. Some are doing really well. They're probably in the top 10 percent, 15 percent of all Americans in terms of wealth.

We have looked at 10 years and 20 years; let's really go for the grand finale here. Let's say that you invested for 30 years. Imagine that you have a new born baby and you want to make sure that your child will do well so you decide to invest five dollars a day for that baby for 30 years. Let's look at that number. The person who invests would have $281,349 dollars when they only invested a total of $54,750. This means that $226,599 comes from interest. Paradoxically, that's money that they did *not earn*. That's money that almost seemingly came out of nowhere. Can you imagine what would have happened if that money had been spent instead of invested?

This is why I wanted to write this quick guide, or mini-book. Of course, you can read a more in-depth 300 page book, but simplicity is best, especially when it comes to wealth building. If you know someone who is afraid of the stock market, show him/her these numbers. You may not believe me, but numbers don't lie.

Help them understand that if you simply saved five dollars a day for 30 years in a traditional savings account, you'd have $54,000. That's great and I am not making light of that. Some people don't invest because they're scared of losing some of that $54,000 but when you don't invest that money, you don't allow your money to *work for you.*

That person just gave away almost a quarter of a million dollars. They literally took a quarter of a million dollars and threw it down the toilet or threw it in the garbage. The thing about investing is that the history of the stock market says that there's been no 20 year period and no 30 year period in American history where a person engaged in very basic investing strategies, like a diversified portfolio, has lost money.

It's never happened. If people diversified and they never lost money then what are we scared of? Yes, there is day to day fluctuations in the market. The market fluctuates on a daily basis, but over the long term, the trend of the stock market (since 191) is to go up, up, up, up, up, up, up over any decade. You're not going to see any decade where it just goes down, down, down.

It doesn't do that. Even the Great Depression was a great chance for people to make a ton of money because they waited it out. They did not pull their money, but they waited for the market to calm down.

CHAPTER 4

NEXT STEPS: WHAT NOW?

Investing is a lot like picking clothes. It's like one's style. Maybe you like jeans and I like something else, corduroy or something. Does anybody wear corduroy anymore or did I just sound really old when I wrote that? Remember, the world is changing. You can reshape your paradigm and your approach based on the existing opportunities that are out there or you can stay locked in the past which means that several opportunities will elude you. You can't live in 2017 with a 1992 mindset; that's not going to work. It's just not going to work for you.

Think of it this way. Anything that you can predict based on information, can be looked up in a magazine or a book. Remember that millions of other people have that same information. Because of this, prices change based on the information.

Let's say, for example, there's information in *Time Magazine* that says that General Electric is going to make an extra $10 billion a year next year, and you say,

"Oh my God, I just read that GE is going to be making all this money. I'm going to go buy some GE stock."

Well, by the time you go back and buy it, the price would have already changed to reflect that information. Investors would have already pushed the price up. So you're paying more for that company because it's a more valuable company because of this information that's been released. That's what they call the efficient markets hypothesis, which leads to what they call the random walk theory in finance.

I won't go into either of these in greater detail because my goal is to guide you in a way that's going to make sense. I just wanted you be aware of those terms in case you decide to do further research. In fact, I created *theblackstockmarketprogram.com* to address questions that I cannot cover in this book.

As you reflect back over the information that I shared in this guide, I want you to think about your current relationship with money. What should you do differently? And how will your decisions determine your children's relationship with money?

In fact, we want you to make the commitment so we have created an investment club. You can go to the drboyceinvestmentclub.com and you can just sign up. We'll give you updates and information. At some point, we'll even send out a survey to see how many of you are sticking with the plan.

This is something that I think can make a measurable tectonic shift in black wealth. I have examined the wealth gap over time and I know some people believe that we can't catch up with white people because white people, by the time we've all got our extra quarter million in wealth, will have had a lot more wealth growth. Their money would have grown too. Here's the thing, half of all white people don't even invest in the stock market. That's the first thing. Only about 48 percent of all Americans participate in the stock market which is a huge mistake.

Second, over the last 30 years, white wealth has only grown by about 30 to 40 percent. If you go out 30 years, white wealth is projected to be less than 200 thousand dollars in total—keep in mind that this is family wealth, not per capita or individual.

The five dollar a day plan is built for the individual. If you have a family of five and all five of you do it, then that means that instead of $289,000 you're looking at a much larger number. You would be looking at 1.4 million. At 1.4 million dollars, your family is doing extremely well, better than the median white family, and even better than the median white college educated family.

This brings me to my next point. A lot of you can afford more than five dollars a day. A lot of us waste more than five dollars a day. Rather than calling this the five dollar day investment plan, I encourage you to call it the 10 dollar a day investment plan. Let's see what happens if you invest 10 dollars a day over 30 years. You will earn half a million dollars; $453,000 of which is interest.

This is why Einstein, a mathematical genius, flipped out over the power of compound interest. He said, I do not understand how money can grow so fast just because you've invested it. When you don't invest, you're losing money. To put it bluntly, as I have mentioned before, you're throwing money away.

Stop thinking that you can't do it. You can do it. Don't be afraid. It's out there for you. If you want to join our investment club, we can help. If you do this, it does not benefit me, it benefits you. If you want to build in your life, I encourage you to go hard, but if you can't go hard right now then go soft. Just make sure that you're going. That's the key. You have to invest. You can't just sit still because when you sit still, other people get ahead of you.

I also want to encourage you to sign up at blackfinancialliteracy.com. Talk to your family about it. Let them read this. Help them understand that we need to let go of this lie that says if you're born poor, you have to stay poor. Or that you need money to make money. I just showed you that you only need a little bit of money to start the process. Growing large amounts of wealth is like starting a forest fire. A forest fire can start from the spark of a tiny match.

Money is the same way. The spark of just a little bit of money a day—as long as you're consistent—can grow into massive amounts of money if you stick with the plan. To be fair, if you don't stick with the plan then you're going to have a problem. Like anything of value, it is important to learn about it and trust the process.

Like everyone else, I started with a blank canvas. I had to decide what I wanted to paint, the colors I wanted to use, and who I wanted to invite to the table with me. I did not create a masterpiece on my first try, so I had to keep painting, even if it meant grabbing a new canvas and starting over sometimes.

Where ever you are in your journey, do not get discouraged and do not feel like you have to do this alone. $5 a day, one day at a time.

Peace.

ABOUT THE AUTHOR

Dr. Boyce D. Watkins is one of the leading financial scholars and social commentators in America. He advocates for education, economic empowerment and social justice and has changed the definition of what it means to be a Black scholar and leader in America.

He is one of the founding fathers of the field of Financial Activism – The objective of creating social change through the use of conscientious capitalism. He is a Blue Ribbon Speaker with Great Black Speakers, Inc. and one of the most highly sought after public figures in the country.

In addition to publishing a multitude of scholarly articles on finance, education and black social commentary, Dr. Watkins has presented his message to millions, making regular appearances in various national media outlets, including CNN, Good Morning America, MSNBC, FOX News, BET, NPR, Essence Magazine, USA Today, The

Today Show, ESPN, The Tom Joyner Morning Show and CBS Sports.

Educationally, Dr. Watkins earned BA and BS degrees with a triple major in Finance, Economics and Business Management. In college, he was selected by the Wall Street Journal as the Outstanding Graduating Senior in Finance. He then earned a Masters Degree in Mathematical Statistics from University of Kentucky and a PhD in Finance from Ohio State University and was the only African-American in the world to earn a PHD in Finance during the year 2002. He is the founder of The Black Wealth Bootcamp, The Black Business School and The Your Black World coalition, which have a collective total of 300,000 subscribers and 1.4 million social media followers world-wide.

In 2017, Simmons College, an HBCU in Kentucky, announced the creation of The Dr. Boyce Watkins Economic Empowerment Institute, where the goal is to develop black economic leaders for the 21st century and beyond.

Dr. Watkins is also the founder of The Black Business School and The Black Wealth Bootcamp, which have over 35,000 students.

Made in the USA
Middletown, DE
24 July 2018